MORNINGS IN THE BALTIC

ADAM THORPE

Secker & Warburg
POETRY

First published in England 1988 by
Martin Secker & Warburg Limited
Michelin House, 81 Fulham Road,
London SW3 6RB

Copyright © Adam Thorpe 1988

British Library Cataloguing in Publication Data

Thorpe, Adam
  Mornings in the Baltic.
  I. Title
  821'.914

ISBN 0-436-52070-2

Printed in Great Britain by
Biddles Ltd, Guildford and King's Lynn

CONTENTS

ACKNOWLEDGEMENTS

Acknowledgements are due to the following:

Bugantics, Literary Review, 1986 National Poetry Competition Anthology, Outposts, Oxford Poetry, Poetry Review, Resurgence, Times Literary Supplement

Some of these poems appeared previously in *New Chatto Poets* (Chatto & Windus) and *The Gregory Poems 1985–1986* (Penguin/ Salamander).

'Neighbours' was commissioned for BBC 'English By Radio'.

'Beeley Brook' won second prize in the 1986 National Poetry Competition.

Note: The four-poem sequence starting with 'Windows' is written in memory of my grandmother, Grace Greenlees (1896–1985). 'Sapphics for my Grandmother' is dedicated to my paternal grandmother, Elizabeth Thorpe, who died in 1981.

Time cannot vanish without trace for it is a subjective, spiritual category; and the time we have lived settles in our soul as an experience placed within time.

ANDREY TARKOVSKY

DRAMA WORKSHOP, AVEBURY

After rehearsals in the village hall
the children took their cymbals, drums,
pipes and whistles, masks and costumes,

out into the centre of the ring
and began the performance: some the spirits
of the forest, some the destruction,

one who refused to be anything other
than his dog. Not much audience:
a gathering of helpers, a German couple

who wondered if it was traditional,
the local custom. No, I said.
There was a light drizzle, and the sheep

ignored us. The few upright stones
leaned like those old, kindly men
in parks, always vaguely interested

in what is going on. The ridge
swept round enormous behind the houses.
Drums and cymbals and humming and cries

and one eight-year-old running
to the ridged horizon, instead
of turning for the happy finale.

She explained afterwards, dazed and panting –
'there's too much space,' sweeping her hand;
and returned to orange in plastic cups.

EGG PACKING STATION,
WILTSHIRE

It's difficult to find anything
interesting to say about it:
I read Lawrence's *Apocalypse*
between the boxes, those short breaks

which on Waitrose days were few,
if ever; his attack on St Francis
hovering unread in the middle
of its sentence as the lids

slid into the cardboard exterior
and the tape twisted to seal it
from the tape-cutter. Sometimes
the lids ran out, or the labels

gummed together, or the tape
refused to cut at the flick of the wrist
(an acquired skill) and yards of it
would web as the belt crammed with boxes.

It got me excited, *Apocalypse*:
sweeps of history obliterated
almost completely the chatter
of the perpetual radio, its speaker

vying manfully with the regular
bass of the sorter and the belt's rumble,
the shrieks and laughter of the personnel
typing letters on the heads of eggs

as they coffined them in sixes, each bubbling
down the sorter to oblivion. Until
the supervisor tapped my shoulder
as supervisors have done for millennia

and informed me that reading was forbidden.
Apocalypse-less, I grew depressed
at the expectation of an eternity
of eggs; even the buzzer failed

to cheer me: crouched over tea
in the fogged canteen, the news of the village
excluded as code does. I read
the backs of crisp-packets, learning

about the longest car in the world
or the record for log-rolling, who
survived the highest fall, landing
in deep snow without a parachute.

There was Mike, sixteen, not
considering anything but this
'because the Bomb'll drop.' Sue
who I stumbled into as she was kissing

Ellen, ginger and androgynous,
in the doorway after the shift
with frost already thick on the road.
I liked all of them: and after

walking alone on the chalk downland
their voices were warm, and their laughter
something unassailable. Each night
at the end, tired and aching,

we mopped up the broken ones
that failed to make it: yolks and albumen
swirled into buckets, like some
terrible abortion, apocalyptical.

We were, of course, tender with our own:
each cradled a dozen (we had them cheaper)
in a queue to clock our cards at nine
in the machine, and out into

air like a thirst of iced water
drinking us up: walking past
the management consultant's thatched
cottage with its Lautrec poster

and pinewood furniture we stopped
to wrap our coats closer: snow
all over the downs to Marlborough,
the blackthorn exact in the swing of headlamps.

THE DRUMMER, 1476

We need you, Drummer of Niklashausen,
who rose from piping in the hostelries
and hearing your tabor echo in the squares of the Tauber,
who left your flock milling in the fields
sloping to the village, tinkling
their neck-bells, the day you were told

how the eloquence of that Franciscan
Giovanni di Capistrano
had brought the crowds swilling through the streets after him;
Hans Bohm burnt his drum
and now commands eleven pages
in Norman Cohn's *The Pursuit of the Millennium*,

the usual pattern of the revolutionary
'suddenly able to command
astonishing eloquence', seized by hysterical pilgrims
for bits of his clothes like John Lennon,
razing authority in a version
of the new Millennium and promising brotherhood,

free rights to wood and pasturage,
the abolition of property, hunting
and fishing for all, priests and emperors divested of purple;
the aid of the Virgin in a radiant vision
establishing his authority.
Imprisoned eventually (forty pilgrims

shot attempting to rescue him),
he burnt as well as the wood
and skin of his tabor did, the vast hordes silent,
expecting a miracle. The ashes
sinking slowly in the current of the river
to avoid a reliquary, while some

scooped the earth charred
at the foot of the stake, 'and treasured that.'
The historical unravelling in the aftermath
is appropriately seedy: local lords
said to have exploited him
to overthrow the Bishop of Wurzburg,

the parish priest eager for offerings
inventing miracles, a local hermit
prompting Bohm the shepherd-boy like a better Rasputin.
The hundreds of offerings piled
at the foot of the statue of the Virgin
shared between the local count

and Bishop, and the Archbishop of Mainz, who razed
the church. Would it have been better, Hans,
to have stayed half-witted and piped and drummed, to have led
    your flock
at dawn through the dewy tussocks
and survived to see your grandchild dance
than preach stark naked in a tavern,

or face a sea of upturned faces
waving their banners and singing in unison
'O Man of God, sent from Heaven, take pity on us!'

CARTILIDGE IN HONDURAS

It was after the first strike
we reached the rubber plantation;
months of rain had annulled
the tracks from their configuration:

abandoned lorries were bivouacs
for vests with children somehow in them,
and the leaves had rotted. We drove
past a shuttered mansion with hydrangeas.

On and on, until the mountains froze
our diary entries with *Yea, Arrived.*
We were glad of the end of the villages,
shacks with cans and Coca-Cola signs.

We built our Mission and waited for the Indians.
They arrived in twos and threes, not singly,
and were baptised in return for food,
in pitiful condition from the common cold

sown by traders. More of them had died
from something brought by a documentary film-crew –
AIDS, possibly. Or perhaps the flu.
At any rate, most of them were saved by us

before we buried them. Nothing I could say
or do would persuade the medicine man.
He launched the counter-attack from his stool
in the courtyard of the village, haranguing

us in tongues young Desmond knew
were not decipherable, because invented.
We read the Bible in a little circle
and he pissed against us; our patience grew

thin and we shouted, *C'mon, man, the hour
has come!* – but he spun round on his toes and hoovered
half the air in with a great cry
so animal we looked toward the forest.

How he'd gone in that little time
with all his masks and bells and feather
we glanced away we never knew, but sure
as this great church stands where he stood

(or danced, as he was never exactly still)
the dust just hung with the heat, and where
his feet were . . . dreadful smooth . . . the dust
shifted its cloud into our open mouths.

THE COLLECTION

(Berkshire County Council Refuse Department)

Vast the estates we would conquer, replete with corruption.
Harvests stooked in a stench of their rotting, fruit
splay-footed, the cats vomiting. Our soldier would hurl
the anthelion of shield at the shins of birch, or twirl

the lids across tweeded lawns to shock the convolvulus.
The going was hard, though eased by necessity:
our shoulders bumped by the plundered steel, its rim
unthreading the weft of muscle. Fires' remnants

stuffed into cans (their ash the heft of a ton
of sofa) clogged the lungs as we shuddered them free
at the cart's lip; legends of fingers clipped
at the knuckle by the falling blade, the sprays of blood

patterning the yellow with their fleur-de-lis. And corpses,
freed of their iron cocoons, abandoned embalmed
in the dawn frost. There was beauty in it:
a fragrance of wine from a broken bottle, a child

sleepy at the netted window, a brass-buttoned coat
in its ghost of polythene, a lidless kettle. Or a manual,
rain-warped, laid gently on the chest, urging us
page after page to love . . . Or slivers of glass

leaved in swords like the offering of horns
round the Neanderthal child near the city of Samarkand;
while the living prepared for our next arrival
in the silence of houses, trussing their dead.

CLIFFS AT DOVER

The black-backed gulls remember Caesar; wheel and shriek
where England's sawn like blubber,
and a grass-blade designates

enough, surveys
the unmapped kingdom of wind and water.
Behind is a clutter

of shops and hospitals, the granite
definitions of northernness,
a washing-line loud in the Hebrides.

Here, surprised, England looks up
her viridian skirts, discovering
the albuminous pallor of dead invertebrates,

the schoolroom instrument of empire.

THE HAND-AXE, c.135,000 BC

*(La Cotte du St Brelade, Jersey; in memory of
Professor Charles McBurney)*

Dawn finds us crouched in coughs of trowels or puff
of brush as mammoth-skull is manicured
to air; the sea trembles its phlegm on the cave's
mouth – our palms pressed to murmurings of bone

string staves to shrew's fibula, monstrous horn,
the jaws of reindeer. This hearth yields leaves
in flint and quartz, its warm millennia
recalled in countless rings of ash; each

inch peels the wind's howl that drummed the waves
to tundra, or the flame that flickered and danced
Homo sapiens neanderthalensis
on the anonymity of world.

Under the sedge that flings at the cliff's lip
our mammoth's skull enfolds a boulder, cracked
to brains they sucked for warmth from the ice wind.
My steel clicks: stone fathoms its new continent.

Prised from its suck of clod, laved in foam,
the greenstone hand-axe floats our cloudless sky
on its ocean film; what eye do I touch,
after such silence, that is not my own?

She was dark, gypsy, on her way
to the Camargue. Somewhere near Bourges
as I remember
was the lost opportunity:
months of galloping on horses, and she
dark-skinned, with an obvious ability
to break them, the sun
dallying on her T-shirt, which was thin.

Smo-o-o-ke on the wa-a-ter
from the little speaker above the door
outside; the *guardien* brought out
an enormous basket of cherries, then another;
when he was gone
it was just the two of us, popping in cherries
like a Boucher.
The dust of the courtyard
was swept by my toes under the table.

Fresh out of school
my French was A-level, the situation
not one they ever gave you in the oral.
I wanted to go with her,
and as cherry after cherry was popped
in between her reddening lips
I attempted to talk about horses,
searching for the word for 'gallop', or even

'mane'.
In my delirium (the baskets
growing emptier and emptier),
I realised that my description of my riding lessons
had been applied to hair.
Actually, she was grumpy, her lips
pulled down
and she hardly ever looked at me.

When the last
cherry lay forlornly rotten
and the bowl was full of stones
the *guardien* (a hippy),
changed the tape to
Riders on the Storm and came out to sit with us.
Later I played *boules*
with a bloke my age who'd just left *le militaire*.

She went to bed
early.
I still imagined some miraculous
transformation would occur;
that down the long, empty dormitory
she'd come, dark-skinned and lithe
wanting me
to rein her in. All I dreamt about

was hair,
and in the morning
over bread the bloke I'd played *boules* with
talked about his plans to be an engineer.
She'd gone,
early. I mounted
the saddle of my Puch moped
and bowled on down the long, empty D-roads of Berry.

BEELEY BROOK

What it says is baby-talk for
meeting the river this afternoon;
pushy, loud, it ignores the moorland
for secret plantations of pine and conifer,
wetting walkers on stepping-stones
skirted with willowmoss, smooth and slippery.
Yet one's untouched, still warm with sun,
a single, enormous slab the brook
slaps at and pleads to muscle round:
someone's scored its gritstone flank with
KATH I LOVE YOU, embracing rain.

Worn somewhat, it's lost its punch,
prey to buttocks and studded boots
as well as the elements: each
hopping bird a finger to the lips!
In a few centuries, if I was still around
and the brook no bigger, and the slab
in place and the slopes around still
uninhabited, I'd scrabble down and find
the terse profundity of stone restored,
the casual, unencumbered hieroglyphs
of age and weather; not a trace of passion.

But what does it matter? Kath, anyway,
is probably gone, from the wear of her name;
and the hand of her lover tugged by nettles
in some local cemetery, or consumed in flame.
But ah – what a setting for your memorial, Kath!
No gravestone tells of those brief lunacies
we compass our lives by – the fact that so-and-so
(a name, a date) was worth grinding at gritstone for:
that the way in which she swayed as she walked, the manner
of her turning and her simple laughter, sent
men to slabs to scour their ardour –

as this does, Kath, over and over!

THE CITY OF THE CIRCLE
AND THE SQUARE

(sculpture by Eduardo Paolozzi, Tate Gallery)

Five thousand years after Mesopotamia
you boast the wheel we invented: our carts
trading with the Indus. Your pillar starts
from the temple at Uruk, each a diameter

of eight foot from the mud of the Tigris,
sunned to brick. Your aluminium
sings at a hit: hollow from the drum
of the gods you lack, and of the lit metropolis.

Our realm rustled to marsh and water, each god
skied in tiered Ziggurat, freed
from monotony; that murmured in the reeds
dream of Ishtar, of love and of war! Flood

mumbled through barley to the walls of Ur,
reclaiming the mud of her. We knew she was never
the eternal city, but the seed of an endeavour
century after century, the chirr

of crickets drowned by gongs, the squeak of pottery.
We, too, were pinned by our pillars in the final
emergency, unable to turn. Our streets are lines
string tautens to, or smashed statuary

wiped and glassed, propitiated by
this same reverence you too accord.
Here comes the priest, moistening the floor
with a scalp on a stick, each sweep the sigh

of Enlil moving in the reeds, ignored.

THE DEAD, INCLUDING

We are the *passers-by*
in a time of ricochets,
gathered in our Heaven
of amazing stories,

a humdrum lot
of no proper cohesion
bar the slightly surprised
look, the loss of a life

like a footnote
in some much bigger volume
than we had ever expected.
We all have something

silly to regret:
every pause we made
on that shopping trip
increasingly significant,

every twitch
of acceleration
towards the corner of the road
where the timer whirred

analysed, regretted.
What keeps us busy
is the imagining of what
we might have grown to

had we not emerged
at that precise instant
or stopped at the traffic light
by the bank, the embassy.

We calculate the odds
and think of our family.
Words like 'chance' or 'luck'
are banned: someone

divine must
have led us by the hand
to that precision spot
or if not

thinking that
we would go mad. For
we are the extras of history.
We are, in our own way, important.

TO MY FATHER

One of the ways we communicate
is the Bugatti meeting at Prescott:
father and son wreathed in Castor
and Methanol, somewhat poor relations
between the billowing tents – you selling yours

in '63, unable to pay for its 'restoration'
after years of topping ninety down the Quai d'Orsay.
I stand uncertain in the blue tear-drops
lined for the Concours, the judges
dissembling their preferences in arcane conversation,

you fingering the polished dashboard
of a Type 37, the one day of the year
a private vocabulary is shared – drop-head coupé,
wet multiple plate clutch as a type of transmission,
crankshaft, flywheel, cambox, and the stamp of Molsheim.

Our faces distorted, pulled in the curve
of waxed body-shell the heavens are envious of,
we lean together in a scent of upholstery
the sunlight flexes, its hot leather
breathing a memory of chivalry in the Targa Florio

of '29, Silverstone and Brooklands
and the Mont Ventoux hill-climb.
Pennants flutter above the lunch-tent
as the marshals gather; after our picnic
of Brie and Rivaner, we prop our elbows on the fence

and watch the members 'having a go'
up the hill, puffing the sand at the corners,
double-declutching in a roar
of eight cylinders and rubber. Nothing matters
but how one takes the horseshoe bend and the sudden

ascent. We race each other in the Renault,
you yelling as I spin slightly
to ease perfectly from first to fourth;
both in a blur of trees and people
disputing our respective times, then glad they were equal.

WINDOWS

Stuck for an hour, not unwilling,
I relate the news, how the weather
continues on in scuds beyond the glass
and think that, probably, you'll never again
know that stink of wet collar, or Ambre Solaire.

News dumps its folded message
across your bed: a glimpse of riots
in Birmingham, your horoscope
left unread, too tired to read . . . you dread
not knowing, that is all, not knowing

what comes after this, and the daily dressing
of hip-wound, bed-sore, your ageing body
failing, just, to correspond
and losing unseen in a border war.
You chatter, sleep, wake to pain

and the sudden, and obvious, disappointment
that it's not a dream. I make you sip some Perrier
and glean a grape some grocer lumped
a paper-bag with – that trade outside
oblivious of this trade with something

unseen, cold, but practical.
Rita, McCartney's meter maid,
retires in public on the colour screen:
beamed in here she vies for time
with time's penalties of pain and drip.

The song, as always, remains the same:
Rita, Rita, meter maid . . .
you wake, again, and tell me how
you miss the teaching, even now;
the sunk Titanic, in aquamarine, looms

to view on the colour screen.
You sip some more, your new routine
demanding liquid to stave off death
in renal failure, though you still state
one sip suffices, not fifty more

as the nurse requires. The ward hums
with blue uniforms and the faithful visitor
bearing blooms through the double-doors:
I prop your cards of mountain-tops
and misted chateaux against the water

like tiny windows to a brighter world
that slips down flat at the arrival of supper, a slush
spooned out from lidded trolleys, cauliflower-cheese
your fork tugs at briefly, then's left to sink in . . .
As from this country of sheets and neon

I rise to go, touch your hand and kiss
to wave distant from the double-doors
before, again, this wind and litter
whispers, *yes, you are still alive*
by a hair's breadth, by the crack in the slab.

DEATH-BED

We crouch around on plastic chairs,
grief's topography of stares and chat
not yet yielded to tears beneath.

I'd bought some flowers and photographs
of Gotland beach-slopes, limestone shores
on which – and this I'd planned to tell you –

sea-bed fossils curled in slabs
were stumbled on, three weeks before.
Last night you joked through storms of pain,

gripped the bar above your head
to knuckle clear of the sudden surge
now, this morning, stilled by morphine's

Arctic calm: each breath you draw
plucks one summer from some dark millennium,
our heads tiny in your sightless gaze.

Just half-an-hour, the doctor said: your brow
glints still with oil from the chaplain's thumb;
your dentures in, I half expect

a sudden laugh, some recognition
of feeling daft, and craving tea.
But no, the glacial's setting in

between us, smoothed in a wordless howl.
What drowns my voice as, bending low
I stroke your brow and ask *How are you?* –

lips still warm, too far from this.
The flowers curve in a plastic jug.
The crumbling plaster's blank and huge.

Two men come in with tools and ladder . . .
'That's the one.' And rattle the glass
in the window-frame, check the sash

that's bust and cough, still blind to us.
'You're starting now?' They turn and nod.
'But this,' I state, 'is a death-bed.'

They stare, astonished; then mumbling, go.
All work has ceased. All small endeavours
retreat before your paling breath;

you'll leave behind your few possessions,
perfume, toothbrush, two frayed settees . . .
We wait, stumbling up our memories of you,

each strata witness to your glittering seas.

NIGHT-DUTY

You died alone
as the nurse phoned us.
2.30. The dangerous hour
in the midst of a city
slowed to sleep, one gutter-

drip. We drove,
it seemed, in slow-motion,
no movie-score annulling what
some script had made
immense, significant, each wet

pavement vast
with colour, blossoming
the traffic-light. Ten minutes
late, and nebulae between us . . .
or God perhaps, the corridor jeering

our footsteps back
in the lit silence. The doctor billowed
apologetic towards us; the nurse
said she'd 'tidy up –
a cup of tea?' We waited where

ash had settled on a torn settee.
Tucked up, neat, what would she be?
A futile vessel? A stiller version
of that which morphine
had already made her –

someone appallingly old,
asleep? Loss had not yet crept its palm
past our sips of sweet tea.
We murmured to ourselves down the corridor
and shuffled in. Dim-lit, bare,

that tatty room
was where, somehow, you begin.
Beyond the sheet's crisp, Alpine hump
your brow rose like a winter moon.
I kissed your cheek. Your head

rocked without resistance,
dull, tepid, uninvolved.
I know now what death is not.
Through a slid-back door a knifed policeman
stared as we left; tucked up, astonished.

ONE IN THREE

As all the viols of Heaven smack
in Ragtime slender bows on strings
to tug you up and through and in

I'm already back in the Hospital,
mumbling to Reception about *her things*:
so Earth continues antiphonally –

for each great blaze of choir above
there's some wheedling, exact response
down here. Near the still-flooded lavatory

and the ashtrays, beneath the hearty mural
of *Dancing Women, Form V11B*
I feel I'm waiting to catalogue

your sins; reduced to nemesis in a room
where raspberries are a thing of the past,
the wind on grass or the sea's fishiness

less than irrelevant, the dying are hardly
ascetic, but fuss dreadfully over pleasures
one hand can count. So the carrier

bag arrives, its *Patient's Property*
an ironic pun: you'd rather
have waited even longer, not fussed by

boredom to that extent . . .
And who can blame you? That last time you were
compos mentis, seething with pain,

you still confessed a worry only
that all was not quite right, the first
inkling in three long months and just

three days over. I'm asked to tick
each item off: have you advanced
to the throne's foot yet? *One talc,*

one toothbrush, one tin of mints. Not
a fanfare from a sea of brass
could more rejoice in you than these!

And yet . . . and yet . . . what doesn't make them
the merely tawdry, the pathetic,
the unbearably intimate scroll that knocks

against my knees as I stride to Ladbroke
Grove through the blown litter? I don't
know, to be honest, despite the aroma

that wafts upwards and makes me think
you're walking beside me, joking, giggling,
admonishing the dog-turds and the weather.

CAMARGUE

In the tall, cold, Victorian classroom
with its windows fixed so no-one could see
anything interesting to distract them,

hunched beside the empty desk still innocently
sloped for Timothy – who'd slid off Snowdon
banging his pick-axe in the handle-end

and bumped six hundred feet too far
from us and this classroom – I'd stare at the one
tacked image of freedom . . . three white horses

planing the endless shallows of the sunned
Camargue. The photographer was somehow above them –
flying, no doubt. The water had hidden the land,

so it seemed as if the horses galloped on the weight
of ocean, foamed where each of their hooves hit it.
Wind in their manes, and the eight letters of the name

a simple kind of spell on the peeled wall . . .
CAMARGUE. We finally went there, last year,
and the sun had dried the marshes up so mud

popped and burbled, or cracked its flats. A couple
from Paris got their Citroën stuck, she
immaculately hopping like a stork

in her white dress; he peeled to his underpants
slipping and floundering around the wheel like a Sumo
wrestler, black to his neck, shovelling bark

under the rutted tyre, grunting with anger.
A passing warden of the *Parc National*
shrugged one shoulder, a prophetic deity

weary of the struggles of humanity. Five
thousand francs, he pouted, if they happened
to be caught by a *Parc* policeman. He tossed his head –

et vous aussi, pour les aider! The heat
shimmered on the Vaccarès. We slapped at gnats
as the woman hopped, attempting take-off in a blur

of hands, her lipstick blooming begonia-red.
Eventually a Range-Rover towed them out,
a great gouge spun from the smooth marsh-bed.

And all the horses we saw were ridden, tin-cans
littering the hoof-marked flats, drained of disguise.
Each night we were bitten, swarms rising from the gorse

of the camp-site. We finally walked the beach from Stes-
Maries-de-la-Mer, striding through sand with the wind
on our nakedness, the world suddenly unafraid

of its first frailties, glorying in skin. We smacked
through foam; entered yelling the warmth of ocean
the soaring universe bumps its rump on.

NEIGHBOURS

My mother noticed it first, that smell
the day before her yearly garden
barbecue; lemon soufflés
in the fridge, the wobble of trifle.
For days before she'd scanned the skies
as July wilted the dahlias, steamed
in the field left fallow behind.

The stench grew serious; by dusk
we had our fists to mouths, wondered
if the blue, rather beautiful ribbons
rippling in the thistles at the back
had anything to do with it.
We strolled to the wire of the garden,
saw through the draped convolvulus

the intimate colours of our neighbours
displayed on the field; the loud
ecstasy of flies above
what glittering clarity! – the tissue
scrolled amongst thistles, small gules
of cotton-wool, the fesse of the organic.
We stumbled back and my mother

spat, feeling her health go. Me
and my father trooped round in a column;
they yelled back about a blockage
in the septic tank, and brimming bowls.
It failed to rain, but the wind
veered somewhat, towards the wood.

When they came we told each not
to look beyond the wire. One
by one, in the middle of some bright
conversation, balancing their wine
on a plate of sausages and steak,
they'd glance, quickly, then turn their heads back,
the smile still frozen on their mouths.

THE HUNT

The agonies we went through.
The crawling on ice.
The hard, polar fist
Dismissing the packdog's eyes.

Each spoor we trembled to touch
Had melted by morning,
Or blown away
In fine dust.

All track lost
By the time the mountains
Shifted their loads of snow.
Trapped by the river's snowmelt

Slipping in spasms
We forded the stones: the yeti
Vanished:
Silence of cloud and mountain.

We took too long. The sun
Hammered our skulls to shape.
We broke our flints.
We forgot what it was we'd come here for.

Clothes shredded, we grappled for skins
With puma and hare.
We dreamt of fire, not knowing
The exact procedure.

The hunt was over. Our dreams revolved
Around the shattered skulls
Of shrew and mammoth: and they
Too rare, encased in ice

On the broad tundra.
Our jaws
Grew stronger, our minds
Simpler,

Settled to strange rest.
We loved one another at night,
And in the morning
Called

To the four walls of the valley,
Hearing the silence
Pitch at our claws,
Our thick and terrible clothing of hair.

MORNINGS IN THE BALTIC

(Gotland, Sweden)

Assuming as always
that unrigidity, the God-fearing shape
unleashed to drowned sunlight
and stones bedded on sand
the Baltic cold endures us like some summer burn.

Bare as eels
we slide, tongue Slavic currents
the glide of Viking prows
foamed momentarily
into Hel's half-corpse claws, the wake of the conquered.

Off this lonely
island, its bouldered, pine-darkened shore
we bob as twin indentations
on something fashioned
for the whole world's rough embrace, for fiddlers to glorify . . .

we need a voice
pure as the ululating wind
was sidling through our sleep last night
in the dark tent
if we are, as seems unlikely, not to be summoned.

We make for shore
too numb to endure much more
and as we towel dry I remember
the ferry over, the dancers
twirling to the old songs on its tiny, flat roof

and the silent waters all around.

BOWLING

Click, click: the runners on the time-belt
stilled into nothing more than a dream
the green sward bumpily complies with.

Age is immaculate: the scene concocted
out of mild dyspepsia, the sudden growth
into chuckles like a distant weir; time

fobbed off along the run somewhere this
green their destiny, the bold rolled
into grave afternoons of humour, boredom.

From here the old men look as if they lean
in preparation for flight, while the scene
as a whole suspends upon a ball

all the possible futures that can come.

MEMORIAL TO THE RESISTANCE

(Volterra, Tuscany)

These faces bear our appraisal with patience;
embossed in rows on the stone wall they've grown
heraldic: some with the timid look of family
photographs: others formal, or blurred as if drowned.

They are guileless, being legendary.
They smile, and seem more ignorant than us
of betrayal; they are the gallery of those
we would have liked to have become, approaching

the borders of our failure. Most of them are young.
They manœuvre for a place in the general massacre
above the legend of each name; the currency of smiles
vie with one another, or succumb to rain.

Once as children they called and the walls answered,
over and over; now shouldering its stone
they gaze upon the old, on what they might have become
in the secrecy of days, down the shuttered streets.

THE SECOND COMING

Each morning I walk it: about a mile
of track, through downland tilth, to
four, rather lonely-looking barrows;
clamber up the tussocks of the one the Victorians

failed to attack with picks and pince-nez
and let November reel over plough-line
and pasture . . . few trees to bother it, so
the solitary pine nearby's a surge

clear as if the breakers rolled, not fields.
I sit on the settlings of marine organisms
from the Upper Cretaceous; chuck a flint
whose conchoidal fracture made it suit

the need for scrapers and sacrificial knives
some years back. The population here
was bigger then. It begins to rain.
I've traced on the map the longest ley-line

and found, amazed, that on its way
from Bury St Edmunds to St Michael's Mount
it bumps one hundred yards or so
past that barrow, there, and on

to Avebury, Stonehenge, and the Glastonbury Tor.
It all fits in. That's why I'm here!
I read *Resurgence* by oil-lamp: sleep
under thatch. Have cut down weeds and planted

strawberries. Smear my cheeks with Wiltshire
sod (after closing time), and shout
to Sirius, and the Plough I can recognise.
I've always heard it's dangerous here. And now

this! It's said to be (in that Atlantis book)
the route He'll take when He returns. Each year
some bread's left out, in case. He'll have a job:
ignoring Footpaths, all Rights of Way,

it slams through brick on vast estates,
'll cake His boots with chalk and clay.
I imagine Him now, the cold breeze
here parting His donkey-jacket, fluttering

His scarf like a Union banner
as He pauses, sniffing, somewhere peopleless.
Practical, of course, to deal with
pharmaceutical industries and all

the ins-and-outs of Common Law and what
to do when unemployed or starving under
an Oxfam blanket, He'll have a map in a clear
plastic envelope about his neck, and

several pairs of socks. And'll know exactly
what's tucked up beneath my rump now
damp in tussocks: which stubbled king
or wrinkled mother, what elk-tooth pendant or beaker

stippled with the origins of the Universe.
I see Him turn and clamber down
to my favourite beech-wood the line skewers
and which, though small, is a kind of cathedral

deer take to, scattering their scuts
at the first footfall; though they're all
slobber and muzzling of palms now He's
gone in. Not quite St Francis He'll scatter the rooks

not, from the sound of it (or the look
for that matter, hunch-backed and tattered)
quite on His side – although I may be wrong.
And then He appears in the further field

heading inexorably towards the M4's
distant flicker . . . no junction to respect
our county lore. A dwindling figure, whose face
and even colour I've somehow forgotten, just

a back bobbed over wastes of flint, hands
thrust in pockets, and a deer
trotting. That's it, then; no laying on of hands
for yours truly. My fibrositis

still the same (worse when driving)
I gaze at the Giant's Grave that sprouts
on the horizon its beard of oaks
and on which, yesterday, I stumbled on skulls

of sheep, tens of them, that must have died
in a blizzard. And somewhat chilled
myself at the thought of it, scramble
down and run to the beech-wood

where, of course, no deer are to be seen.

DIARY

Square-rigged, one hundred and eighty tons, ninety feet from stern to tip, our Stilla Maris
hums across the chop of landward water
the shore embezzles. The scent of battened pine
is fine. Our knives click on the wooden platters.

Forty-seven are lowered this first winter;
we share our meals with Wampanoags. March:
from out the interior a Pemaquid stumbles,
mumbling peace . . . we have seeded our affliction
and the Lord provides. Our first crop roots in the mouths

of the dead, where we have buried them. Squanto
touches the bread and sucks his thumbs. Right now
I hear the pebbled stream through the clicks of firelight,
the squeak of Standish rubbing his guns. I dream,
sometimes, of Leyden: cuffs laid white across

the blood of oranges, plums pulped in children's
mouths down the loud streets. And May, they say,
is the unlucky month; it flowered to this
under its wide lugs: starlight, sea-breezes,
something certain in the sight of our children.

Alden touched his foot first on the foamed rock.
I shall be forgotten; but He provides.

Plymouth, New England, 1621

PUTTING THE BOOT IN

Oar-stuck, the grave
marked for custody

someone's boots,
knees, cranium.

There was a watch
all night but no-one

saw; the spirit
moored in the reeds

had either freed
itself or not;

we weren't too sure
of anything.

Dawn came
with peewits, gloves

over hands and all
the crap armour

we'd been buckled
into having.

As we left
someone broke it

beneath the blade:
it was rotten,

had stayed upright
God knows how

many wars
and winters. We came

across the remnants
of the opposition:

holed up in caves,
their plumes had faded.

We put the boot in,
saved on blades.

O HOW I REMEMBER

Hivac, the neon-
bulb factory I spent a vacation in,
its rhythm clicking my tongue long after
I had left it.

Fumes like bubble-gum,
molten glass pinched on the rim of a drum
and the dipped filaments; one morning
it grabbed the thumb

of the neighbouring operator:
blood jetting in a high fountain
we cleared with mops. Evenings in the stilled
woodlands, taut with frost,

stars and leaf-mould. Chesham
glittering in orange and amber, the valley
where the Chilternsaeten's tribal huts
smoked in a similar cold.

O how I remember
stumbling the nettled survival
of Grim's Dyke; wandering the woods where bodgers
turned once their chairs' legs

on a lathe by a hovel:
the last of the woodlanders waking
at dawn in a scent of their chippings – the soft
alburnum of their living.

FIRST EPIPHANY

(Villa d'Este, Rome)

Though timeless, the present lords it
over the remembered moment, that particular second
we reconcile our boredom to

obscurely memorable.
At thirteen I had no name
for something I considered unnameable:

and while some claim that nothing is anything
until it is named, and vice
versa, I venture it proved the nonsense

of innocence; the sense that everything
is always old and utterly experienced
the litmus test of eternity – that dipped in time

turns deeper than red, or Rilke's *Wolle die Wandlung*! –
the cry to be Changed.
What happened, then, by the Roman pool

ringed by statues astounded, apparently,
at their own noselessness,
lifting their hands in surprise

at the green lizards runnelling over them
neither the lap of the water nor the sun shimmering
had more to do with than was usual;

the slung camera bouncing on the paunch
of a distant American
essential to the predicate

time confirmed by declaring its nullity –
as matter likewise, dissolving
in the liquid of forgotten lives

to something pale now puffing from a toga
on painted tiles, beside the statues'
perfection of magenta; who

loosening a quince-pip from a difficult molar
slides slowly
to the ribbed cool of the pool's water.

Such was the nature of my first
epiphany: not gods exactly but a Roman
consul; hearing what he thought

was a boy's footfall, hearing
the tick of a camera, a sudden flutter by the cedar –
paused, or pauses, caught in a sentence

tenseless; afraid of assassins.

ON LEAVE

Well – we heard a rumble and a cough before us
and a hauling-in of cloaks, rich it was
but dim-hushed, and on approach we stenched
a sweetness:

hemp-seed burnt in a cauldron-censer
(bronze, birch-hugged handles) – sends
y'mind and blows y'chin-strap does it half!
We took 'em

then without a whimper. Well – y'know
the soggy grain we found near Camulodunum
with all the dead-'uns deep in the clunch-pit,
the clasp

you pocketed, the gold molar? It were
the rising of the brain, like when Poenius-boy
boiled it rotten and Cerilius tossed up his guts
on the shield-

leather. Like enough to stuff the Ninth
down Paradise-way and screw off the cold
with the twenty crater of mulsum nicked
from harbour.

Like as not you'd suck y'pizzle to get
a whiff of this: not a cowshit-stopped reed-shaft
but a vestal ticklin' y'baubles near the Agrippa –
or the crunch

and the crushed femur
in the lady-killer's ludi
when the rag-tag bursts
around ye!

O friend, I grant
'ye are na blate', but remember the time
we walked the seven hills, and the curlew split
with a sling-shot; you left a string of violets

for Mother,
clambered up the Palatine
where the she-wolf milk was sucked and laughed
like the blood-smeared boys at Lupercalia

dangling
their goat-skin strips, and told me how I should die;
like the haruspices and their fondled livers
littering the slab you peered and saw instead

yourself
curled in the curlew-gut, and blubbered,
and ran to the temple to pray with upturned palms
and incense? Remember, friend, *quod cinis es* –

and sometime unto ashes you must return.

SWEDISH LAPLAND

At Haparanda the Baltic blew
light like white wine down the estuary,
the little summer houses hidden in pine
clapboarded yellow and orange by the brilliant water.

Joggers rounding the forest track
as the sun wobbled and refused to go under
until the hill hid it. My dreams were sunlit
through the zipped tent, one permanent morning of gnats.

We took the train to Lapland: Abisko
nestled in enormous mountains. We camped
in the shadow of a birch, by a clear pool,
in the middle of a world not yet woken to the sound

of the human voice. We browned our sausages
on an oven of flat stones and local
kindling, alone with gnats and the sun
hovering on the white-capped horizon, this time refusing.

We walked in the morning, taking the path
to the Black Lake frilling its foam
in shafts of sun, like the birth of mythology;
you feeling you had stumbled on something foreseen, a return

within. Up on the snowed-on slopes
of the mountain, crossing a stream, we found
discarded antlers, the foetus of a reindeer,
a gully slipping its slabs of snow so we heard it after.

THE CENTRE

He left a biblical reference
in my clarinet case: had played,
after supper, *Summertime*
and promised to write some *good tunes* out
when we all went round to meet

Jacqueline, now seated opposite
on zebra-skin; the quote still folded
under the embouchure clipped inside
the case at my feet: two verses
from *Habbakuk*. After supper

she disappears upstairs, then he
tells me to follow in a minute
or so and leaves us alone to pour
out coffee. *She's Flemish, you know*,
my father says. I mutter that I'd better

go, and climb to find the room
locked he said to meet him in
and knock. The slip of bolts: they stare
triumphant, then tug me in. *This*,
she hisses, *is our centre here!*

Great, I grin, as her eyes go huge;
see shelves stacked with what I think
is music. She spits, close, *Jehovah's
yours!* – both poised like surgeons as I
mumble something about *Summertime*.

He sighs, and scribbles, to pluck at hair with
God made this! Look! And this!
He tugs another. *It's Him, or ashes!*
Then hums, too quick, *When the living
is easy*, pen poised over empty staves.

46

SANCTISSIMA

A vein of porphyry, a cup
held out as witness, the Supper-
time shenanigans of bleary
breakfastless parishioners

swell into a blaze
of rhododendrons in a pot
after coffee; a momentary
illumination, a taste

of sanctus, sanctissima,
and the language without endings.
Rose clapped her on the shoulder
and the vicar waved.

All over the world, she thought,
people are so nearly (watch that step)
making themselves holy,
so very, very holy. She wept

through the banging of the doors
of the Ford Granada (the Citroën
never made her sick like this),
and she was gone, Rose said, before the junction.

THE ONLY TIME I HELD
A PYTHON

The only time I held a python
(thirty-foot, in Cameroon)
was by the tail: it shat
in anger, or in fear. And that

was that. Thick and wet, its body
by the human grip allowed
only to defecate
was cold, reptilian power, not hate.

Six held its length, and Charlie took
a photograph. We grin, and look
out of fashion; flared,
long hair. The serpent, where it's bared

between the tiny fists is just
cold, reptilian power, not fussed
by matters of style, the ache
of growing up, or whether to make

the right decisions. (Looking back,
I see how cameras catch my lack
of confidence, my hang-ups
as an adolescent.) The fangs

could pass right through a hand; my father
was on the head. It seemed to lather
at the lips, opened out, its tongue
volatile, thin, and tried to lunge

from the hot steadiness that kept it
from the ground. Its fear or anger leapt
uselessly and this was sad,
somehow. And that's when it dribbled, smelt bad.

SCARECROW

Condemned to this most vulnerable of gestures –
wings stretched, head caught skywards,
the suppleness of chest and heart unguarded –

out of the frost-starched feathers
its bone rises, scoured of accretions
the scrubbings of wind have garnered.

An autumnal morning, the cold still wintering
the tops of fence-posts, sugaring the wire
its neck is noosed to – the smell expelled

useless over the stubble. The worms
perform their delicate surgeries, turning
corpse to anatomy, body to soil

somehow, while the wire clings
to its offering of sky. Examine the machinery
of joint and socket, the nostril's filigree

where the cry reverberated: astonishing,
how an ugliness of feathers puckering its carrion
reveals to this; pale, pure, like the bell

of a snowdrop on its gravity of spine.
Or a word hacked through meaning after meaning –
shiphook, lever, the claws of time

on the eyelid's corner, or the cup of the fritillary –
arrived at last at the murmur of its end,
unintelligible as the groan of prayer.

CONDITIONS

The noise that in this glen
coarse-grains the quartzed granite
listens also: it is the condition of silence
that noise needles it, as light
does the tangled murmur of burn.

And being alone is willed
from friends' voices, from whom his leaving
bestowed a kind of tacit recognition
of the conditions of friendship:
an inconversability.

And the glen dreams, not
of the gradual nature of the reign
that's scoured it, nor the husky successions
of its heather, but whatever
he does not dream, it dreams.

MEMORIALS OF WAR

(Piedmont, Italian Alps, 1984)

A walk that war made more than strange:
a jeep-door peeled from its flak of leaves
revealing an afterthought of jacket:
a satchel strung crumbling on its skeleton of wire
and cans peppered by a passing rage
we could play the Crusades in.

There was something truculent about it:
machines brooding on their legends of grass,
cogged crests disavowing senility –
despair at their seized anatomies
and emptied bowels. As if whoever
left here in a hurry

contrived to make it plain how war bored him.
A cable strung down the steep valley
sagged and hummed; some soldier had wound it
round an anchor of fir-trunk, that minute by minute
tightens its bite on the dead wire,
as if to swallow it.

SIDELINES

'I never have sought the world; the world was not to seek me.'
(S. Johnson)

The pair were extraordinary: singled
out from the hunkered types at the bar
by a kind of distance, a willingness to listen,

each was a story from the sidelines, mingled
with a fierce purpose; Alan with his scar
across the temple, and Percy with his mission.

We'd murmur all evening in the corner;
Alan, in his fifties, with his tie and stammer
scrawling slow capitals on strips of pad

and handing them to me with enormous
authority; snatches of Lamb, Johnson, the grammar
erratic but the sense sententious, while a sad

old voice in my ear would enumerate
the sins of capital, a Farm Labourer's Complaint
that in right-wing Wiltshire was a little crazy –

the great Swing riots were *agin the State*
and recent for Percy; since then a taint
had fallen on the others – their memory hazy

of 1830 and the *Rights of Man* . . .
he'd glance around with suspicion and disdain
or simple fear that he'd been overheard

as my pockets would slowly fill with Lamb,
Euripides or Gibbon; an inexhaustible train
of pithy maxims through the blur of words.

Alan had had some operation
on his brain, spent half his life in a ward
for the gently insane; Percy'd ploughed and harrowed

harbouring his leftward inclination
under the bee-line furrows, the hay that poured
through his lungs for half a century, the load

of the labourer. And now they clung
to a long-haired graduate who wrote, and ran
a little company with puppets, whose dreams were rural

in an urban century: a flung-
together trio of the sad who began
to cohere there somehow, and make solitude plural.

WITNESS

Out of kilter what with
drubbings in Tunisia
and the sand as hot as irons

our regimental tracks
were not all that they were
cracked up to be

by wireless operators, mis-
information in the lee of dunes
where 'holed up' did for 'lolled'

as piety for saving face.
Whenever an attack
burnt up some tent

or rapped on the turrets
we'd double the number
and throw in some heroics.

We were pretty all in,
damn tired, sick of dying
men and their futilities.

I used to tap
facts out like dotty
aunts do in Stow–

on-the-Wold, or Stroud.
Then I turned to lying.
My forte was a kind

of quiet hyperbole.
All the officers were stubbled
and had runny eyes

but in the land of the telegraph
they were all *V FIT STOP*.
I had an ear for history.

PILGRIMS

(bound for Canada)

Those moments nothing is but what is wrong
remember Vatesay, the Hebridean
island of moors and car-hulks, white-scrubbed sands
beyond the stones of duns; on which a somewhat
worn granite monument in dune-grass tongues
the fact that even God once had enough
of faith and pilgrims – assuming it was Him
who cut them short by several thousand miles
and flapped their sail-cloth, tossed them round a bit
to grind on rock and hurl them aft for crofters'
fund of outrageous stories: how the wrack
was flesh and crinoline, black-stockinged men
with sober faces; and how for days and days
the bibles floated in, like someone's laughter.

NATURE STUDIES

Raring to go, amused
by summer, the chrysalis
broke open, flew from the jam-jar

an ivory petal.
The emptied vessel
stank of grass, of someone's breath

too long withheld.
The cress, too, grew fat
and lazy, from stubble to beard

on the coal-bunker.
From Woolworth seed
these dahlias have risen

bigger than fists, red
and swollen. An orange tree
in a pot by the sink

winks tiny fruit, three
sucked hearts of gobstoppers
on spindly leaves.

I'm graduating to terrapins,
the next order, with brains
and an inkling of love.

The shells must not go soft,
they like bananas.
Summer will see them

bask on the crazy-paving
in a riot of creation
all made by me, aged ten-and-a-quarter.

Grass, trees, butterflies,
a litter
of emptied jam-jars.

Rabbits are easy, as long
as you watch the foxes – and then,
in a special tank, I'd like

to grow a whale, creaming
the heated water so that
the neighbours would notice

its glittering spume arc high
in the Buckinghamshire sky.
What next? Well, looking in the mirror

I reckon
I could have a go at that,
when I'm older.

ZEBRA, A

Girded round by loin-cloths,
saved for posterity
by camera, knife, the art
of the taxidermist, it
mounted to the realm of dinner-gongs.

No-one dusts the head
with its halter of walnut and wall.
Marble-eyed, it terrifies
generations of children
stuffed with salutary reminders.

It will survive us all.
Pop-eyed in dementia, ticking
past in wheelchairs or
terrifically alive on Alka-Seltzer,
the family bores

will barely glance
at the lustreless muzzle,
the mouth prised slightly ajar
in imitation of breath,
the tiny, brass plaque

wind and cigars have darkened
to an unknown tenure . . .
From its kingdom of leaves
blown in through the door
and the sodden umbrella

it comes, hunting us at night
with its lips drawn back –
searching for its hooves
in some forgotten drawer, trophies
of *God* and *Empire*.

THE LANDING, c.1000 BC

Our keel
scratches the shore, the twisted-
wicker girth-lashings
cleated beneath the keel-plank,
the paddles of ash clicked on stone
where the clay stirs.

Our prow
settles in sweet flag. The breeze
thrums the long-fibred
hair-moss rope
that tugs the planked vessel, taut
in ardour, to the reed land.

We lick
our hands where the blisters
burn from the paddles,
or the spring-haired rope
plaited, smoked,
some of it stuffed in the seams

so water-
stopped and luted. But most of it
clutched, sweated on;
for the hand is the hearth of the blood-heat
to the cold line of boat-rope
twisted through.

A SHORT HISTORY OF
THE HUMAN SPECIES

Living in a tired country,
embalmed in the long-term sufferance
of lost objectives,

a stegosaurus
breaks through bracken-fronds,
its history limitless.

A pin descends,
splintering through ferns
to orthoptera.

God has turned
the globe of the world
to satisfy

some celestial craving,
spun the atlas of his mind
to have something

named, for Chrissake!
Now he contemplates
perfecting silence,

cutting the babble
with an Arctic wand,
hovering with his pin

over pylons,
an ephemera of roofs,
poets

keening with
too much to say,
the great ballooning of His Word.

PEDAGOGICS

for Jo

It felt like elopement; over the sleeping
dead of Wiltshire we wooed
each other from the classroom smell
of socks and digestion. We courted
danger, winked across the Common Room's
clink of cups, locked in to secrecy,
the outrageous curriculum of love. Our spies

were public school, fuelled by curiosity,
knew that only a year or two of acne
kept them from whatever they imagined
we were doing. Smelling slightly of soap
they'd loll outside my door
dispassionate as accountants, the City
already there behind the dangling cuffs,

the sudden offerings of their poetry.
I liked your hair, and in Avebury
you went for a pee in the copse
and left me on the ridge in a swoon
thinking of the lynchets I could sink in,
the round barrows I could rest on,
the soft motte of your bottom when

suddenly I glimpsed you and you waved.
The hardest part was avoiding the blush
in the classroom; Monday mornings
over Chaucer, in the fug, right hand
pale and absolute with chalk-dust, the same
that had explored what my thoughts daren't conjure,
I'd plug on regardless, avoiding puns.

MARMOREAL

for my mother

It's *circa* 1957, all the lawns
afflicted with a static of leaves, the streets
still cobbled and angling the Art Deco Citroëns
parked there. The Metro's trains have manual doors;
our windows swing with a shunt of metal

tongue that rocks the glass . . . through the net
the casements need re-painting. Look, the scent
of a courtyard curled with cats, steps
entranced by their stone banisters flanked by
bollards we'll flake climbing on: the worn

balls of the *belle époque*! Open
the courtyard doors; our flat wafts with winds
off the Seine, Mam'selle Boppe bustling in
with flowers for the hell of it. Every morning
you trundle my pram along the Quai d'Orsay

all the way to the Musée Rodin, its gardens
littered with bits of Carrara, marmoreal.
Look, I am getting used to my appendages
of fists amid blanket and monument; rock
in the wordless despair of incontinence. These smooth

Olympian chins pass, unabashed
by dribble, the emergent struggle from snot and the tang
of saliva from your handkerchief: Think
or Kiss undisturbed by the leaves' crackle.
Effloresced on the surface of my vision

they begin to harden, more dependable
than flesh. One turns slowly as we bump
towards it: torso wracked, each bled eyeball
blank and wide round its drilled retina:
the gaze of the immortal! You start to hum

some Georges Brassens to swathe the clamour of me
and the bronze agony of the Burghers of Calais,
ridiculed by pigeon-shit. The borders of my vision
shift uncontrollably: our maternal diptych
already, for example, near the murmur of the Quai

approaching the empire of the vast Pont
d'Alexandre-Trois, its streaked viridian of lamp
and cherub towering over us. Each subject it carries
I exact a smile from: while something silvery
moves ceaselessly beneath them, ignoring me.

PARADISO

It was Heaven, alright:
we gambolled vaguely about
the first few days, plucked apple-blossom
and wondered where our fat had gone
and the imperfect figure
I'd grown improvidently fond of
over years and years;

all our measurements were roughly the same,
the women had perfect breasts
and the men none of that English shoulder
or bottom – the pear-shape had gone
with the baldness and warts;
a sun-tanned homogeneity of sorts
flitted through the leaves

and over the falling lawns, past
endless kidney-shaped ponds
with multi-coloured gravel
we learnt quite soon were jewels
and utterly valueless
in Heaven: seated in the evenings
round a glorious fire

I wondered whether sex
still had a role in a sort of Lawrentian way:
I didn't dare to ask,
and only when I stumbled on a bouncing bottom
did I realise something was up,
if you get my drift.
Did you take your pick?

Since everyone looked roughly the same
I hared off to chat
with whoever happened to be gambolling nearest
on that balmy night:
as I ran I thought
this is a bit of alright,
years of frustration in a bed-sit rewarded.

A gorgeous group were
murmuring about Kierkegaard or something
and humming folk-tunes.
The only man, I joined in rather
like I used to at the Edmonton Socials
where everyone knew each other
as couples

and before I could lick
the honey off my chin
from the night's repast
(no fixed time for meals, it was all
hunter-gathering)
someone giggled and the lot
tumbled on top of me, everything swinging.

Actually, it was a little
too much. A sort of glut
of all the film-stars you've ever fancied
in the time it takes to suck
your Orange Mivvi
in the trailers. I ran
off, to be honest, over dewy tussocks

to muse on why
my claustrophobia
(I'd fainted, once, in the scrum at school
when it collapsed on top – lifts
would make me shudder
and I felt like swooning on the Tube)
had not been dealt with

like my sloping chin had, my rolls of fat,
my feet. I spent another week
gambolling heartily around
and generally joining in with the sing-songs
and was garlanded with reams of flowers
but all desire (in *that* sense)
was subsumed in worry

that nothing had been done
about my phobias.
Everyone else seemed happy.
I began to retreat into solitude, and wandered
one whole day
without spotting a soul.
Who should I see? I mused,

ready to flap around and sport
if anyone passed me.
The sunlight glittered on the blossom,
which was always dewy.
I thought, *This is Heaven, and I'm
still not perfectly happy,*
and that depressed me even more, quite frankly.

Things got worse.
I brought it up when partnering somebody
in Oranges and Lemons
but he only giggled. He shouted out
This chap says he's a little, well, depressed!
and everyone's mouth became
a great dark hole instead of teeth.

It was a bit like
the time I'd scored a try
(my first) and turned to face
a cheering opposition – we'd changed
sides at half-time and I hadn't noticed.
I was still a weed
and I ran off over tussocks that time, too.

I began to pine for my bed-sit,
the High Street in Edmonton, the dog-shit
and drizzle. Endless boughs flickered over me
and birds carolled and the breeze
was perfumed with something rather like
that stuff I bought in Duty-Free
for Mum (which she never used)

and I gambolled unconvincingly
until I broke
down, weeping, in the conservatory
(pure gold and silver, with unbreakable glass)
and the whole place froze.
Their jaws dropped. Their gambols
were sort of suspended, arms half up,

wobbling on a leg.
A thunder-clap.
I had clearly failed
to impress some chap up top,
whose generosity was famous, who'd overlooked
quite a lot
when it came to the decision over me.

I was immediately cold. All those
Scandinaviany types
merged into a grey
sort of soupy fog. Things cleared a bit
and there it was:
Hell.
Where

you belong, some voice
intoned.
A few rather tawdry-looking shops,
a high-rise in a drizzle, an old
woman and a rolling bottle
and religious graffiti
(God's a Dosser, Sod Off God)

and I walked
all day in my anorak
unable to contain
my irrepressible delight
that I could drag my heels and slope
along hunched up,
my eternal dream of fitting in

finally arrived at.

THE ADVISER

It is his whispers still my blood.
I remember the lizard. I remember
The lilies he fingered, the ghosted pond
And the pyre's gust of my grandmother.

Everything turns; everything bends.
His thirst distends in times
Of storm. I remember the lizard.
I remember the taunts of friends.

My throne trembles to desert dust.
The toads quiver. He reads
That I should rise again
With scarlet fingers, to smear the just.

Everything turns; everything bends.
The moons rise and songs are sung
As memories round desert flame:
He fingers lilies, and still pretends

The precept of freedom is genius.

BACHELORS

The chalky dynasties of learning
are lost on the fly
throttling up against imponderable glass;

a cloakroom smell of discarded coats,
socked feet unheeled
from plimsolls, generally abrades the atmosphere

in which the teacher is declaiming
Ted Hughes's *Thistles*
thinking half the time of Amanda's breasts

under the check-cloth on his left.
He's avant-garde,
fronting his desk, the class around him like a henge,

lounged over copies of *The New Poetry*,
the tough kind, good,
that when he ends sends not a pellet winging

but giggles at *stiff with weapons* (rude).
Next door, by chance,
(a drone just discernible through the plywood partition)

five rows of pupils and an elderly man
are listening to
Betjeman's *Upper Lambourne*, recorded in nineteen-

sixty-three, bobbing on the gramophone
usefully portable
when he bought it all those years back in Chingford.

When the bell rings the discussions
end in the middle,
almost simultaneously, and the Sirs collide

without touching in the corridor.
Each rides his notions
like a motorbike, mild-manneredly greeting the other

through a soundless roar of disdain
as the wide roads open
up to the throttle and they cleave the years

alone, unstoppering the sherry.

AN ATLAS

An atlas is utterly quiet, disdaining
anything but names, panoptic brilliance
of the accurate. It sums it all up,

the spurious vigour, the sprawl of shame
on a bed somewhere in Bolivia
or wherever the pin stops. Everything

has happened, and it seems to maintain
the futility of dreams before the facts:
each page dumb to blame, all tact.

MISCARRIAGE

The other women are coming round
or quietly reading, satisfied
that something's mending, tended by
the itch that reassures. We talk

as if in church, you cradled by
hospital pillows, I by nothing
more than your hand in mine, relief
that at least loss takes with it the waiting.

For you, of course, it's different;
you look as from a secret place
of suffering down, and I embrace
a stealthy knowledge, breathe in your hair

of century after century, this
that all of man has cause to stare
and stare at, think: this spot of blood
upon the linen's hers, not mine –

I share the loss as witness, not
as victim. This is what it takes
to keep things going. Bowl after bowl
of brimmed injustice; not quite right.

THE THERAPEUTIC MASSEUR

for Gerry

It is the oldest medicine:
they use their feet in the Punjab, here
his palms clap and pummel

the knotty thongs
of mind.
Some come craving to be touched,

others with the simple
urge to clarify, to assuage
the fury of a body,

a lifetime's tryst with disappointment.
Dancers, poets, priests,
monks whose sex springs up

at the first touch,
pensioners who giggle
and the lonely wives

he smooths into solitude, the knowledge
that this is the sum of their flesh,
and they must love it.

His thumb delves into bleak biographies,
the pages of the body
flutter open to the terrible chapter

that bent the spine
and gave her headaches; the patient
screams to be read.

And day after day
each spreads naked with the blinds drawn down
in the whirr of the heater,

committed to this
outrageous planer of flesh,
hear through the dark

whole shelves collapse
rotten with worm, floor after floor
float down slowly

like parchment
or snow on some high mountain,
or gulls lifting

and falling over great seas.

THE DUN

for my sister, Emma

Seemed hardly worth the trek to see across
the scree and moorland of the Atlantic cliff;
blown down to boulders, little more than rubble,
it's granted status by the Norse hands
that erected it in self-defence,
a look-out post upon a wealth of sea.
Couched in sedge amongst embattled flowers,
shrines to endeavour, each stone lay just
where the wind had put it, legends of a kind
we could wander through in our orange
anoraks, deafened by the wind
that slapped us. Induced by the edge, we marked the end
of Scotland with our chins, still rapt by foam's
far-down concussion, the far-off landfall of Iceland.

THE TREE NURSERY

Handling lawson at eight in the morning,
frost rigorous on the miniature stems;
a blackbird practising its octaves, scorning
our pursed lips fluting extempore

snatches of advertising jingles, the opening
bars of Elgar's Cello Concerto.
We ease the oak into its envelope
of loam, thumb the bristles flared

from its twig-trunk home to moistness,
row upon row; each quietly preparing
its forested future, solemn-voiced
on a slope of downland, outwearing

the centuries. No wonder, then,
Johnson's observation: *men,*
when exhorted to plant a tree, begin
to think of dying. A fug of paraffin

in the shed we retire to, crouched over
garibaldis and the *Sporting Times,*
coffee defying the stink of stove
our gloves hang from in paradigms

of fingers' exhaustion. Paul admitting
he's into Milton, then donning his visor
and tank of paraquat, spitting
spray in slow advance up the rise

of *Fagus sylvatica*, or Common
Beech. Following lunch the radio's
propped for Woman's Hour; our pogrom
of weeds through a talk on embryos,

aphids crawling like minions, beetles
in viridian and magenta, a whirr
of ladybirds in amorous twins – the elite
in the tickling kingdom of conifer.

Five, and the blackbird strums in elms
still managing to whisper from the wind-
break. I wheel my moped through realms
I dream of at night – undisciplined

then in forests to be lost in,
now striped up the hill in their fuzz
of infancy: a vast tiger-skin
fleshing slowly as the rain nuzzles.

ARCHAEOLOGIST

He will always have
ravines in his granite headland,
a rock to sit on with his vacuum flask
and a bright anorak
from the chilled spindrift at the sea-mouth.
Staves of string, the taut map
that pretends to order
what is casual providence,
blots on the sketch-book.

His farts linger
above the spear-heads'
erratic domesticity, buried at the hearth
and by the mammoth-bone still thundered in nightmare.
One day
the loll of a jaw
will surprise him, its gaze of socket.
His wife and children at home, thinking
how quiet the big chair sits without him,
how clear the air.

NAVAHO

(after a photograph by Edward S. Curtis)

His thumbs pressed us to sleep in the long trays.
We drifted through memories of mountains, the liquid
Stung our eyes:

We thought we were drowned. Then sudden we awoke
Jewelled, glyptic, numinous, dripping from tongs
The primum materium

That washed our dim remembrances clean
Of the desert's breath, the stench of leather. Etched from silvers,
Swabbed with a sponge,

Our faces are blurred as dreams we half-remember
Under the starlight's vast particulars, under the wind.
I am the woman

Who turns and leans, hair streamed in thin flags,
Lips pulled to a grin by the hook of the shutter; thinking
This might be eternal –

The bedrock clocked by hooves, the moan of the wind,
The stiff ingiving of the saddle. You shuffle past
Our framed freeze,

Omnipotent mooning faces – white, puissant,
Temporal – and pause, sometimes, to flick the catalogue, pin
Us with the sharp

Demotic of name; the wound of the blood's struggle
Cauterised, made clean by letters. I lean to pull
My horse's rein,

Parting the grass to dark's invulnerable hug
As the clouds race, fevered by dusk, and you pass on
In dream after dream after dream.

HOUSE-HUNTING

Pitched in the Neolithic
through the mammoth days of the Dordogne
they never had this trouble, the old
peripatetic tent-dwellers

of our simpler youth.
Antelopes ranged, wild horses and the ubiquitous
bison were chalked
or stencilled on the cave-face;

no-one thought of moving
for any other reason than to eat
or occupy a sacred space
where there was water and a hill.

How beautifully unbourgeois!
Listening to the dulcet tones
of some estate agent
carolling the lux kit/diner and the orig feats

makes me think of tussocks,
skin-flaps pegged against the wind
and the bitterness of smoke
rolling over forest after forest

to where the world ends
abruptly, like a cliff.
Everyone was dark then, and wrinkled . . .
'I've

another one here, newly
available, fit cpts and FGCH . . .'
And so instead of the hearth, in place
of the endless windswept spaces

days of awful decor take
us briefly into other lives
we examine with a sniffy intimacy,
poking into bedrooms, trying to be nice –

ignoring the drawn-back sheets
revealing the stains
and the ashtrays littered
like obsessions between the photographs;

while all of them are desperate
that we shove them out, grab the place where
something might have been achieved
in a different light, but it wasn't.

And what of us? Wondering as we look
if here beyond the dreadful colours
our future could move for good.
And somehow terrified that it might.

Bronze infused from dandelion, petal-stewed, racked
off and bottled: camomile, vellum-scented:
foggy mint. Each year I would clip the lip of
    grass with the giant

shears I'd dwarf now; crumbled the mounds of moles.
Locked chests foamed to crochet and soldiers' postcards,
frothed my thumbs with brooches, or mouldering stares of
    relatives dabbed to

focus: 'Who was that?' 'That's your Uncle Stan.'
'Him?' 'That's Fred; his lungs, we were told, were soft from
gas. He pegged soon after.' His letter, pitying
    'Jerry, who dropped like

stone'. Cathedrals, shattered, on postcards snipped where
rats, it said, had nibbled at corners; Stan's
souvenir of Rheims's unscissored ribs
    bronzed in the snowed-up

sepia. Glassed and framed was the scorch of Father,
silk top-hatted, tossed on the chords you billowed
from the press of bone, your mercurial trill's
    quiver of throat-folds

forking hymns. His Manchester factory stank, you
said, of tar; its brushes unclogging streets of
leaves, or smoothing gulleys of his sulphurous frown.
    Morning unfogged to

Bakewell's moor and golf-course, the Salts next door;
breakfast tutting over the Texas sniper
as the sunlight caught your embroidered homily
    losing its threads. Your

Bible cracked its vast spine; each page slid firm to
Adam, tinted red, in a Congo parkland . . .
Bedtime witnessed ritual unpinning of hair
        coiling its pour of

silver. As you snored through the wall I dreamt it
water. Or rainfall moistening the stones the morning,
later, you were bobbed on a string; a wood
        box to infuse soil.

PILLS

A whole host of reds and blues
had fought it off for years
until the last supper.

She'd had it up to here.
A rock could not have
suffered more the sea

than she the fealty of depression.
Her tits were far too large,
she'd said over coffee.

This was her quaint obsession,
that men could not hug her round
to meet up with their fingers.

I'd said all that was needed
to persuade her that ministrations
were feathers bedraggled in a bucket,

or so she'd maintained with that
curious image. She was either
a poet and a visionary

or a moaner with a lurid
turn of phrase. If the latter
then God bless the emptied bottle.

If I seem cruel, it's only
the anger she's left me with
at being alive; guilt of the imperfect.

ABANDONED CROFT

(Barra, Outer Hebrides)

We entered cautiously, as much as to say
we know you're here, still idling the winds away
by the peat fire; a lonely valley
falling northward to the ocean, the swell of the Atlantic.

It seemed impossible, this far away
from anything southern: the boots waiting
like two sad lepers by the unmade bed,
the mud on them not homely, just forgotten. And the bed

like a plundered tomb, your shape
there like the outline of a coffin, a coffee-stain.
The pillow rucked to the weight of head,
moss crawled up the sheet's mould of thigh-bone and leg.

A taste of turf, the swollen damp of the partition,
stone just shouldering its burden
as it is used to doing. The wind through the window
fluttered the net from its view of moor and ocean.

What caught us most, in the end,
was the letter; kept in place by an Ever-
Ready, it had barely faded: from his daughter, we reckoned,
extolling from the mainland

the virtues of a caravan's Calor heating.
She considered his age and the foolishness of living
in a lonely valley falling to the ocean,
his floor of earth, his turf and stone,

his sheep-pen sagging its thatch to moor . . .
it crumbled when I touched it, like pale fungi.
We stepped outside, blinded by the light,
and walked towards the warrior's tomb on its grassed mountain;

two white stallions, like rags of cloud,
stood amongst the stones of its tumbled dolmen, staring down.
Stumbling up the slope towards them
we wondered if he'd stayed in this lonely valley, calling

after his dwindling flock; until the morning arrived
when someone discovered him, blind
to all he'd clung to. The stallions snort
and roll their eyes and paw

the ground they burst away from
sudden, in a spatter of moor – away
from the sea and the croft and the moor
and we, now tiny, who might have imagined them.